Easter

by Marc Tyler Nobleman

Content Adviser: Alexa Sandmann, Ed.D.,
Professor of Literacy, The University of Toledo;
Member, National Council for the Social Studies

Reading Adviser: Susan Kesselring, M.A., Literacy Educator,
Rosemount-Apple Valley-Eagan (Minnesota) School District

Let's See Library
Compass Point Books
Minneapolis, Minnesota

Compass Point Books
3109 West 50th Street, #115
Minneapolis, MN 55410

Visit Compass Point Books on the Internet at *www.compasspointbooks.com*
or e-mail your request to *custserv@compasspointbooks.com*

On the cover: An Easter basket filled with eggs

Photographs ©: Photri-Microstock/Jack Novak, cover; Stock Montage, Inc., 4; Skjold Photographs, 6; Corbis, 8; Lynda Richardson/Corbis, 10; Mario Tama/Getty Images, 12; Photo Network/Esbin-Anderson, 14; Larry Williams/Corbis, 16; North Wind Picture Archives, 18; Alfredo Estrella/AFP/Getty Images, 20.

Creative Director: Terri Foley
Managing Editor: Catherine Neitge
Editors: Brenda Haugen and Christianne Jones
Photo Researcher: Marcie C. Spence
Designers: Melissa Kes and Les Tranby
Educational Consultant: Diane Smolinski

Library of Congress Cataloging-in-Publication Data
Nobleman, Marc Tyler.
   Easter / by Marc Tyler Nobleman.
      v. cm. — (Let's see)
   Includes bibliographical references and index.
   Contents: What is Easter?—When is Easter?—How did Easter begin?—What happens on Easter?—What other days are associated with Easter?—What are some symbols of Easter?—What do people eat on Easter?—How has Easter changed?—How is Easter observed in other countries?
ISBN 0-7565-0649-2 (hard)
1. Easter. [1. Easter. 2. Holidays.] I. Title. II. Series.
BV55.N63 2004
263'.93—dc22   2003022176

Table of Contents

NOTE: In this book, words that are defined in the glossary
are in **bold** the first time they appear in the text.

What Is Easter?

Easter is a **Christian** holiday. It is sometimes called a feast day or festival.

On Easter, people remember that Jesus Christ came back to life after he died on the cross. His rise from the dead is called the **resurrection**.

Jesus was a teacher and healer. He was born about 2,000 years ago. Jesus had strong ideas that some people did not like, so they killed him. Christians believe Jesus came back to life three days later. They believe Jesus is the son of God.

Christians around the world celebrate Easter. It is the most important day of the year for Christians.

◀ *Jesus Christ carries the cross.*

When Is Easter?

Easter is always on a Sunday, but Easter's exact date changes from year to year. Also, different kinds of Christians have different dates for Easter.

Most Christians celebrate Easter on the first Sunday after the full moon that is on or after March 21. So every year, Easter for them is sometime between March 22 and April 25.

Eastern Orthodox Christians use another type of calendar. They usually celebrate Easter from one to five weeks after other Christians.

◄ *A choir leads other church members in singing Easter songs.*

How Did Easter Begin?

Easter is one of the oldest Christian holidays. Christians started Easter more than 1,800 years ago.

Christians saw that **pagans** had a spring festival. Unlike Christians, pagans believed in more than one god. Their spring festival honored the goddess Eastre. She was the pagans' goddess of spring.

This was the same time of year Christians celebrated Jesus's resurrection. Christians wanted pagans to celebrate Jesus's resurrection, too. So Christians called their celebration Eastre. Over time, some of the pagans became Christians. Later, Christians changed the spelling of the day to Easter.

◄ *A rabbit sits in the green clover near a spring daisy.*

What Happens on Easter?

On Easter Sunday, Christians go to church. They light candles. A priest or pastor leads the church members in celebrating the **Eucharist**. The Eucharist also is called communion. People who take part in the Eucharist eat a **wafer** and sip wine. This reminds people of Jesus's last meal.

The priest or pastor might explain the belief that Jesus came back to life three days after his death. This is a very happy event for Christians. People often get together with family and friends to celebrate after church.

◄ Christians kneel during communion.

What Happens Around Easter?

Lent begins 46 days before Easter. Lent is a time when Christians say prayers. They get ready for Easter. Some **fast**, or eat less, during Lent.

The first day of Lent is called Ash Wednesday. On Ash Wednesday, some people go to church to receive crosses made with ashes on their foreheads. This reminds them of Jesus's cross.

Palm Sunday is one week before Easter. It is the start of Holy Week. Palm branches remind people of the ones that were spread in front of Jesus as he walked to Jerusalem several days before he died.

Good Friday is the Friday before Easter. On Good Friday, people think about the day Jesus died.

◄ *New York police officers with ashes on their foreheads on Ash Wednesday*

What Are Some Symbols of Easter?

One **symbol** of Easter is the Easter Bunny. Long ago, pagans believed rabbits were signs of springtime and the start of new life.

Germans also had the Easter Bunny. In the 1700s, Germans who moved to North America brought the idea of the Easter Bunny with them.

Another Easter symbol is the egg. People colored eggs to celebrate spring. Today, children have egg-rolling contests and egg hunts on Easter.

The white lily is another Easter symbol that stands for new life. Many people buy these flowers to decorate their homes for Easter.

◄ *Children color Easter eggs.*

What Do People Eat on Easter?

People eat many different foods for Easter. Some families eat chicken, turkey, or ham. Others eat roasted lamb. The lamb is a symbol of new life to many religions. The lamb is also a symbol of Jesus.

On Good Friday, people often eat fish. People also enjoy sweet rolls called hot cross buns. On top of each roll is a cross made with white icing. The cross reminds Christians of the cross upon which Jesus died.

Chocolate and other candies also are treats at Easter. Children enjoy chocolates shaped like Easter symbols such as eggs, rabbits, and crosses.

◄ *A family prays before eating a turkey dinner.*

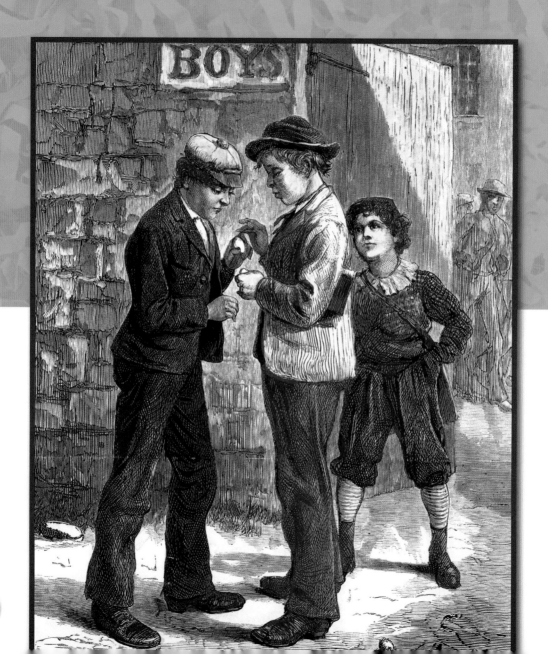

How Has Easter Changed?

At first, people celebrated Easter on different days of the week. Sometimes they celebrated on Friday, sometimes on Saturday, and sometimes on Sunday.

In the fourth century, the Easter rule was created. This rule made Easter happen on a Sunday every year. Christians still follow this rule today.

Hundreds of years ago, people gave colored eggs to servants as gifts. Throughout history, children have received eggs for Easter.

In the past, some Christians could not eat certain foods at all during Lent. Meat, fish, eggs, and milk were not allowed. Today, the food rules are less **strict**.

◄ *Boys crack Easter eggs in the 1870s.*

How Is Easter Observed in Other Countries?

People around the world celebrate Easter in many different ways.

In parts of Africa, people beat on drums while Christian songs are sung. In some countries in Europe, people light **bonfires** on Easter weekend. This is a symbol of winter's end.

In Australia, companies sometimes make chocolate bilbies for Easter. The bilby is an **endangered** animal in Australia. It looks like a rat with big ears.

In Mexico, people light fireworks, and everyone cheers.

All around the world, Easter is a time of joy.

◄ *A man in Mexico celebrates Easter with fireworks.*

Glossary

bonfire—a large outdoor fire

Christian—a person who believes that Jesus Christ is the son of God

endangered—when a kind of animal is in danger of dying out, leaving no more on Earth

Eucharist—a ritual to remember the last meal and death of Jesus Christ

fast—to give up eating food for a short time

pagan—a person whose religion is not Christianity, Judaism, or Islam; a pagan may believe in many gods or none at all

resurrection—the act of coming back to life after death

strict—if a rule is strict, the rule has to be followed in a careful, exact way

symbol—something that stands for something else

wafer—a thin, flat piece of bread

Did You Know?

✳ Some people want Easter to be on the same day every year. They have said the second Sunday in April would be a good day to have Easter.

✳ Easter is connected to the Jewish holiday of Passover. Jesus Christ was Jewish and had his last meal during Passover.

✳ People often wear new clothes on Easter. New Easter clothes are another symbol of new life.

✳ Candles are part of many Easter events. Christians call Jesus "the Light of the World." The light from the candles is a symbol of him. On Good Friday, the day Jesus died, many churches blow out their candles as a symbol that Jesus's light had gone out. On Easter Sunday, the candles are relit to symbolize that Jesus is alive again.

Want to Know More?

In the Library

Carlson, Melody. *Benjamin's Box: A Resurrection Story.* Sisters, Ore.: Gold'n'Honey Books, 1997.

Haugen, Brenda. *Easter.* Minneapolis: Picture Window Books, 2004.

Schuh, Mari C. *Easter.* Mankato, Minn.: Pebble Books, 2003.

Wildsmith, Brian. *The Easter Story.* Grand Rapids, Mich.: Eerdmans Books for Young Readers, 2000.

On the Web

For more information on *Easter,* use FactHound to track down Web sites related to this book.

1. Go to *www.facthound.com*
2. Type in a search word related to this book or this book ID: 0756506492.
3. Click on the *Fetch It* button.

Your trusty FactHound will fetch the best Web sites for you!

On the Road

The Virginia Museum of Fine Arts
Richmond, VA 23221
800/340-1400
To see the Fabergé collection, including some of the famous Fabergé Easter eggs

The Ukrainian Museum
203 Second Ave.
New York, NY 10003
212/228-0110
To see decorated Ukrainian Easter eggs

Index

About the Author

Marc Tyler Nobleman has written more than 40 books for young readers. He has also written for a History Channel show called "The Great American History Quiz" and for several children's magazines including *Nickelodeon*, *Highlights for Children*, and *Read* (a Weekly Reader publication). He is also a cartoonist, and his single panels have appeared in more than 100 magazines internationally. He lives in Connecticut.